# Maths Pack 5
# Area, Perimeter and Volume

This pack belongs to: _____

## Contents

|  | Page Numbers |
|---|---|
| Activity 1: Perimeter | 5 |
| Activity 2: Perimeter and Missing Measurements | 7 |
| Activity 3: Area | 10 |
| Activity 4: Area of Irregular Shapes | 13 |
| Activity 5: Volume | 15 |
| Activity 6: Surface Area | 18 |
| Activity 7: Area and Perimeter | 22 |
| Activity 8: Perimeter Word Problems | 25 |
| Activity 9: Area and Volume Word Problems | 30 |
| Activity 10: Perimeter, Area and Volume Word Problems | 33 |

11Plus Maths Pack 5 – Area, Perimeter and Volume

By KSOL - Aron and Anita Dhunna

A book of challenging 11Plus style Maths questions designed to engage and help children towards the Maths Syllabus used in selection tests.

Published by Key Stages Online Ltd, a company in England and Wales, having a registered company number of 05258999

KSOL is a registered trademark of Key Stages Online Ltd.

First Published 2015

Copyright © Key Stages Online Ltd

Copyright Notice
All rights reserved. No part of this publication may be reproduced in any form or by any means (including photocopying, storing electronically by any means including transient or permanent) without the written permission of the copyright holder Key Stages Online Ltd.

Disclaimer
This material is published by Key Stages Online Ltd, and is an excellent support aid for children who will be sitting an entrance exam. This material does not guarantee a qualification or a pass for any exam. The material should be used as a support aid only. No Liability. Errors and Omissions Excepted.

KSOL is not associated with CEM or the University of Durham in anyway. CEM is a trademark of the University of Durham. Material contained has not been endorsed by CEM or the University of Durham.

ISBN 978-0-9929277-0-7

## General Maths Guidance

Below there are some hints and tips on how to answer the maths problems in this book. Whichever way your child chooses to complete the activities, they must remember to work quickly and carefully.

At the back of the book is a progress chart where you can record your child's results as a percentage and track their progress over each activity.

**You will find the answers in the middle of the workbook. Please remove these before giving the question booklet to your child.**

**Hints and tips:**

- Look at all of the examples provided.

- Familiarise yourself with, and learn all the formulae.

- Be careful when doing calculations and check your answers.

- Make sure that you include units when required.

- Once each activity is completed, ask your parents to go through any incorrect answers with you.

Word Problems

- Read the question and underline the key information, extracting all of the numbers. Don't be put off if there are lots of words.

- Decide which operation to use.

- Solve the problem.

- Check your answer.

- Reread the question, are you calculating exactly what it asks?

## Activity 1: Perimeter

**Example:**

4cm

2cm

The perimeter is the total distance around a shape.
To find the perimeter of a rectangle, calculate the total length of all four sides.
4 x 2 = 8 (There are two sides of 4cm)
2 x 2 = 4 (There are two sides of 2cm)
4 + 8 = 12cm

Find the perimeters of the rectangles below.

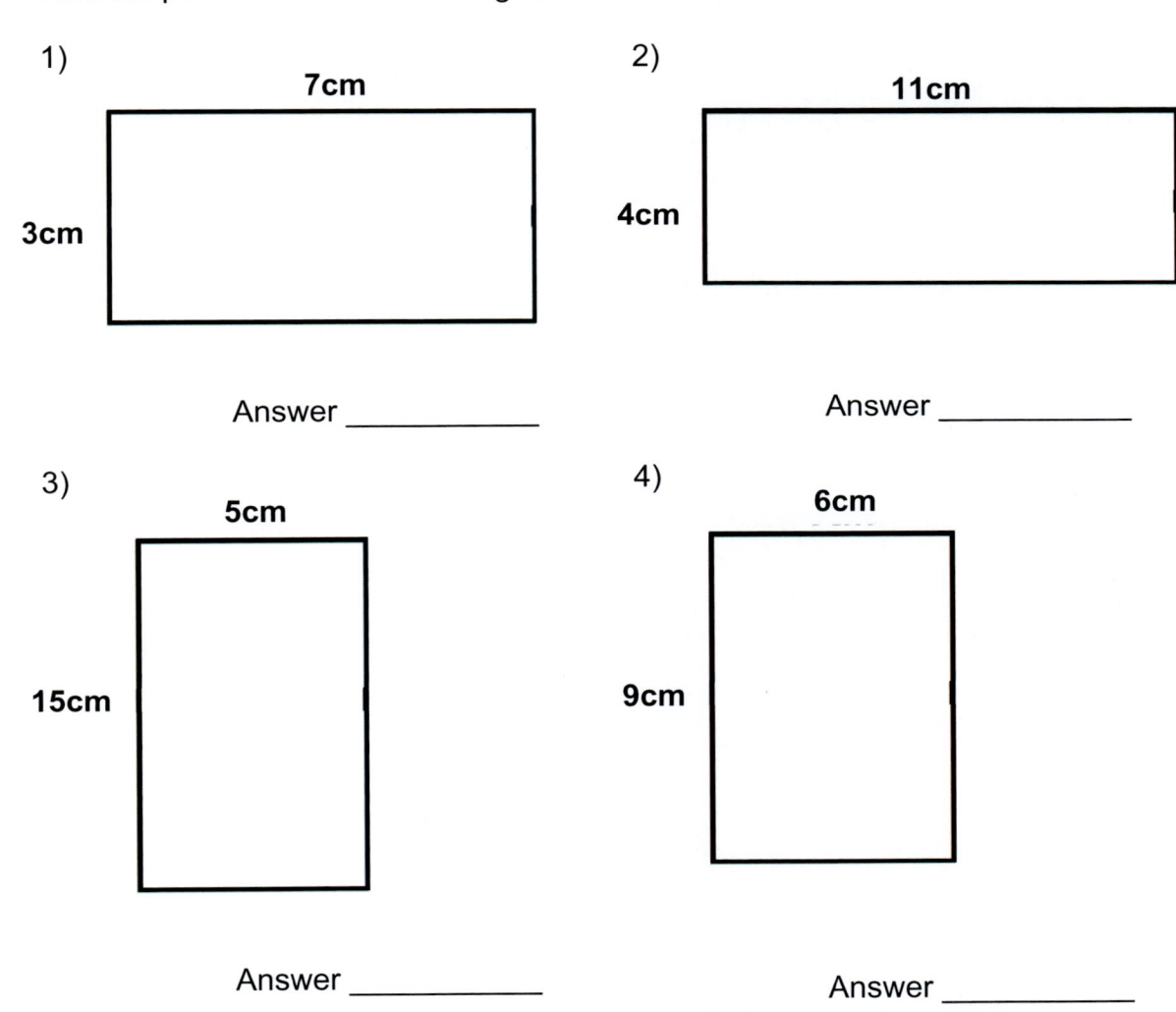

1) 
7cm
3cm

Answer _____

2)
11cm
4cm

Answer _____

3)
5cm
15cm

Answer _____

4)
6cm
9cm

Answer _____

Find the perimeters of the squares below.

5) 6cm

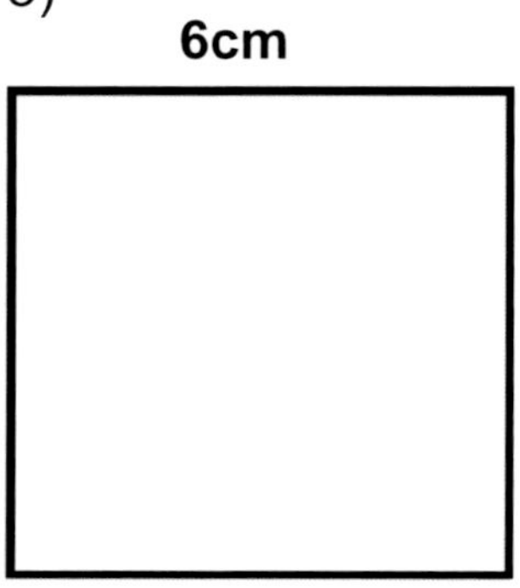

Answer _____

6) 4cm

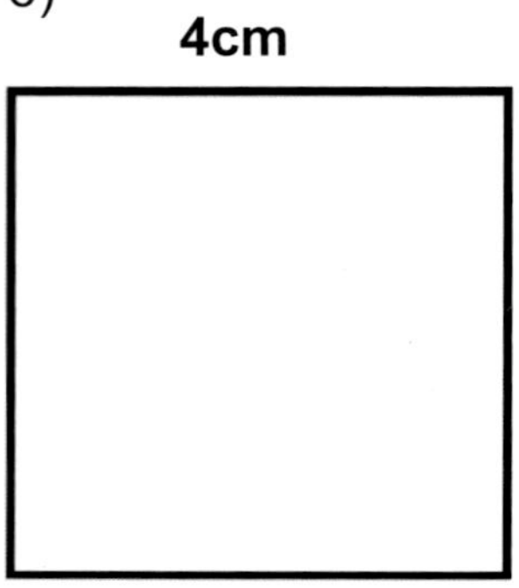

Answer _____

7) 9cm

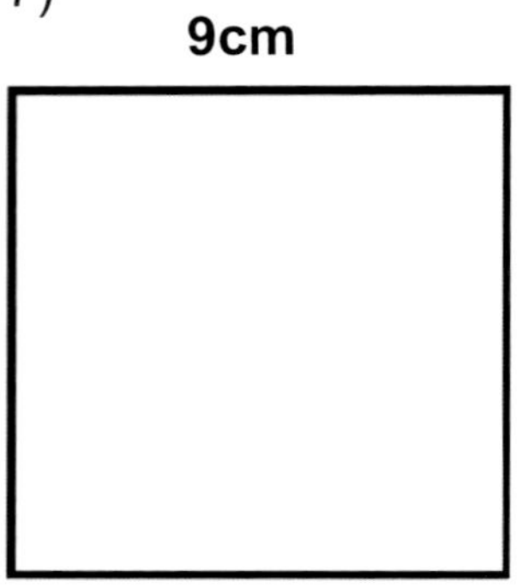

Answer _____

Find the perimeters of the quadrilaterals below.

8) 7cm, 6cm, 9cm, 12cm

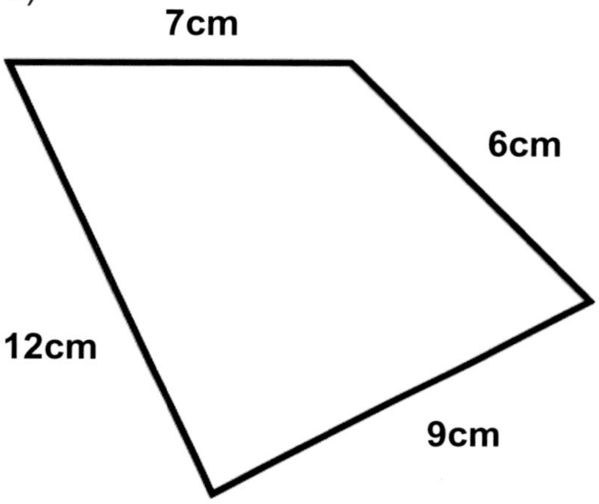

Answer _____

9) 17cm, 7cm, 13cm, 9cm

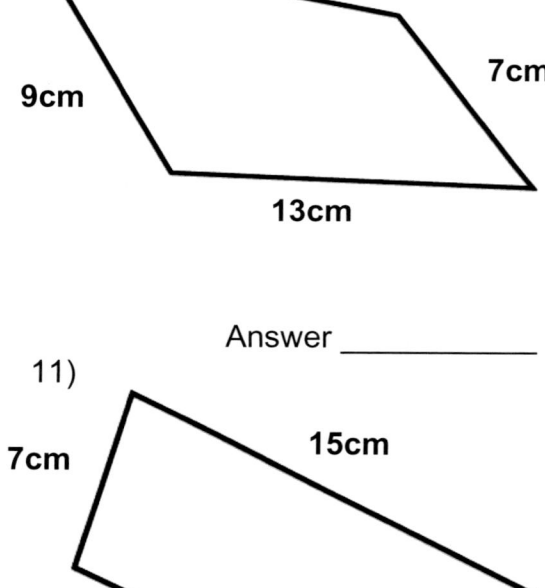

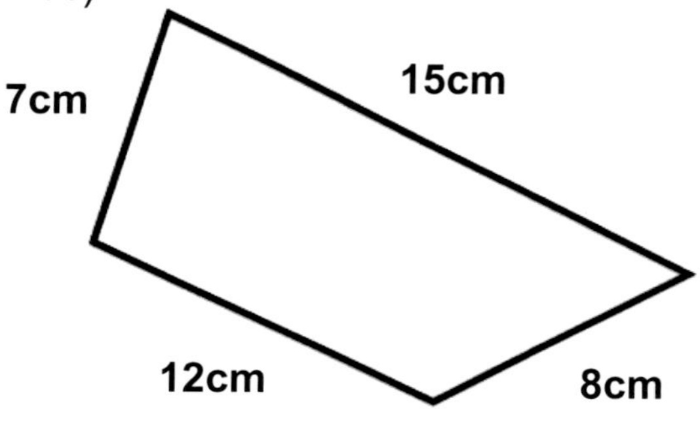

Answer _____

10) 12cm, 2cm, 9cm, 14cm

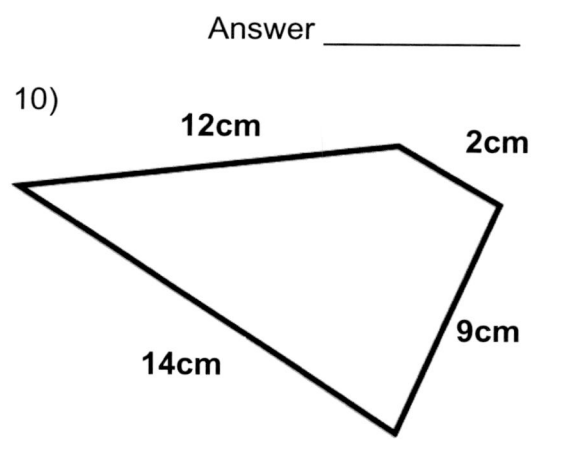

Answer _____

11) 7cm, 15cm, 8cm, 12cm

Answer _____

Total out of 11: _____

## Activity 2: Perimeter and Missing Measurements

**Example:**

Sometimes you won't be given all the measurements you need for the perimeter and you will have to use existing information to work out the rest.

Look at the shape below. The question mark denotes a missing measurement. The dotted line is 2cm and the overall width (at the top) is 6cm, so the missing measurement will be:

6cm − 2cm = 4cm

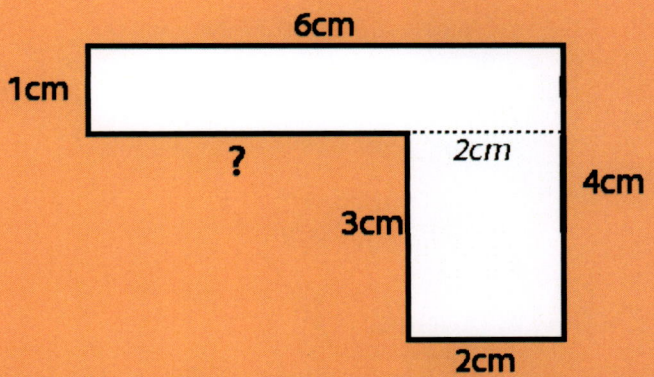

You now have all the measurements needed, so you can work out the perimeter by adding up all the lengths.

Ensure that all measurements have the same units, e.g. cm or mm, before attempting to add them up.

*Note: There will not always be question marks showing missing measurements.*

What are the perimeters of the shapes below?

1)

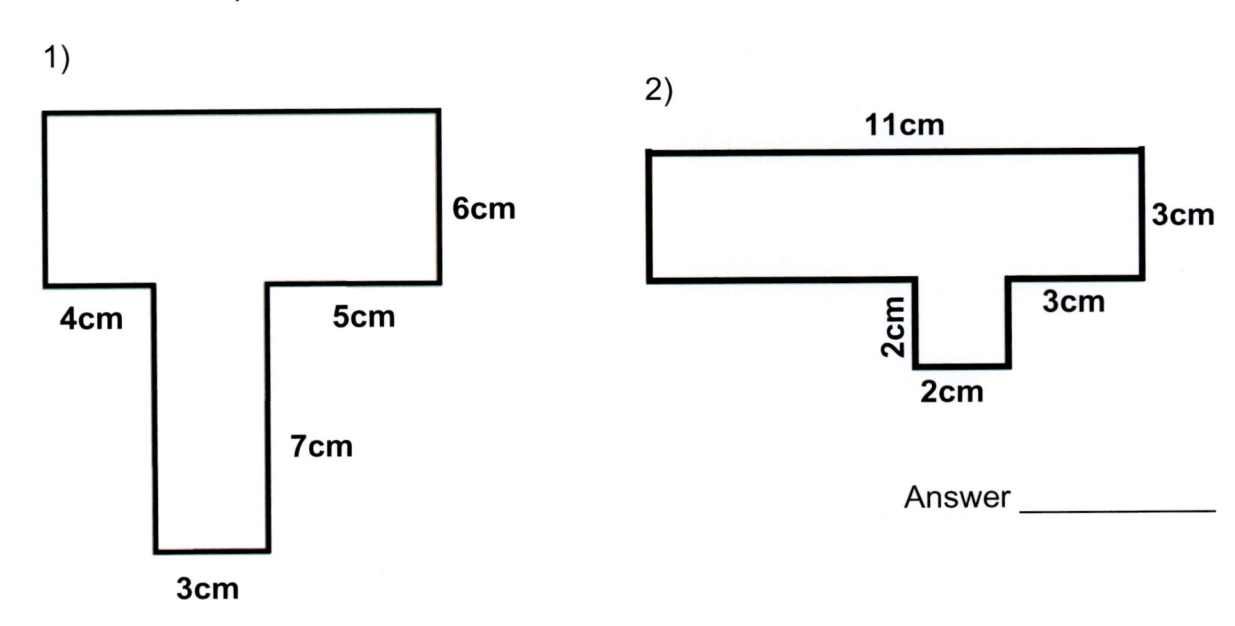

Answer _____

2)

Answer _____

3)

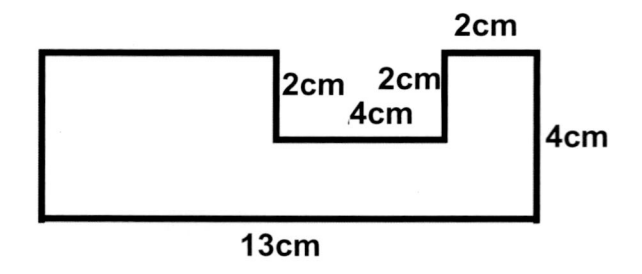

[shape with measurements: 2cm, 2cm, 2cm, 4cm, 4cm, 13cm]

Answer _____

4) The perimeter of this shape is 28cm, what is the value of $x$?

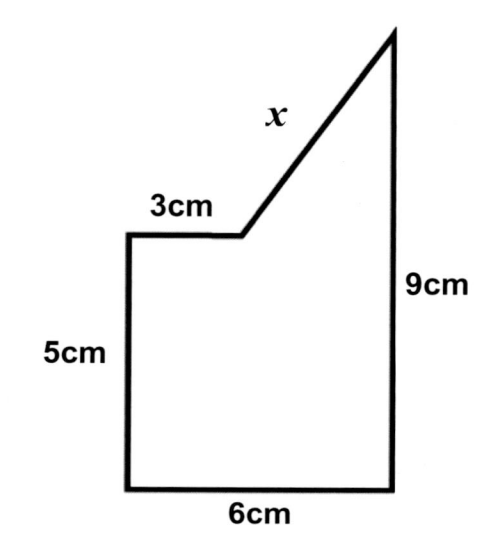

[shape with measurements: $x$, 3cm, 9cm, 5cm, 6cm]

$x$ = _____

5) The perimeter of this shape is 44.5cm, what is the value of $x$?

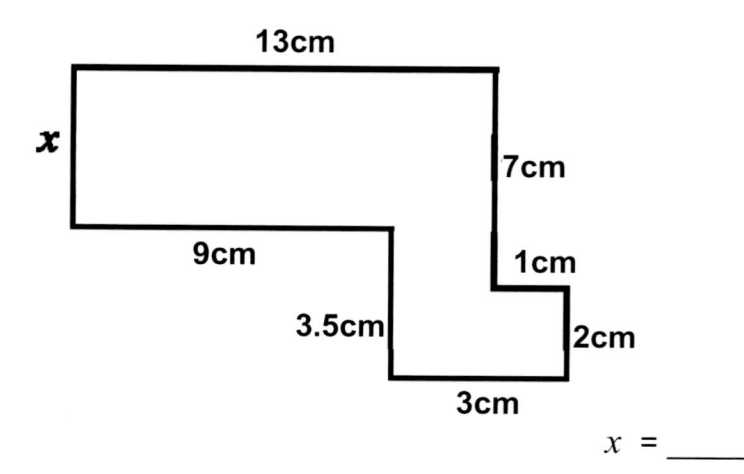

[shape with measurements: 13cm, $x$, 7cm, 9cm, 1cm, 3.5cm, 2cm, 3cm]

$x$ = _____

6) The perimeter of this shape is 19.5cm, what is the value of $x$?

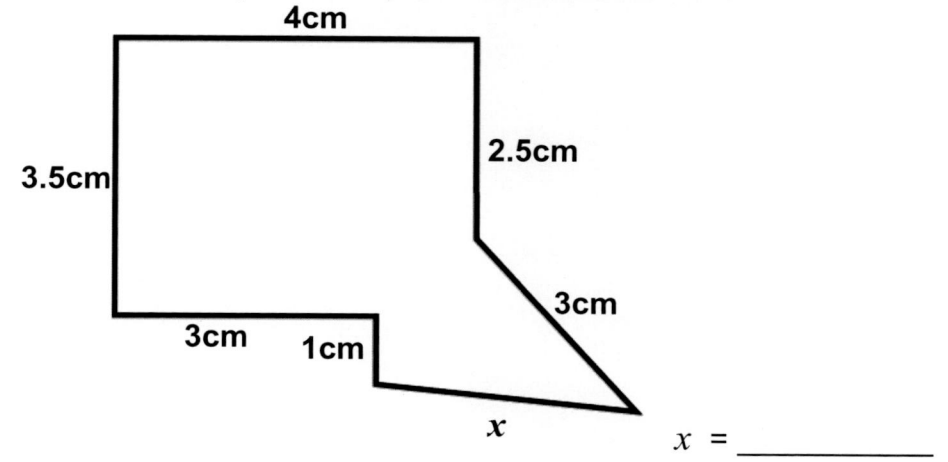

4cm
3.5cm
2.5cm
3cm
3cm
1cm
$x$

$x$ = _____

7) What is the perimeter of the following shape in **cm**?

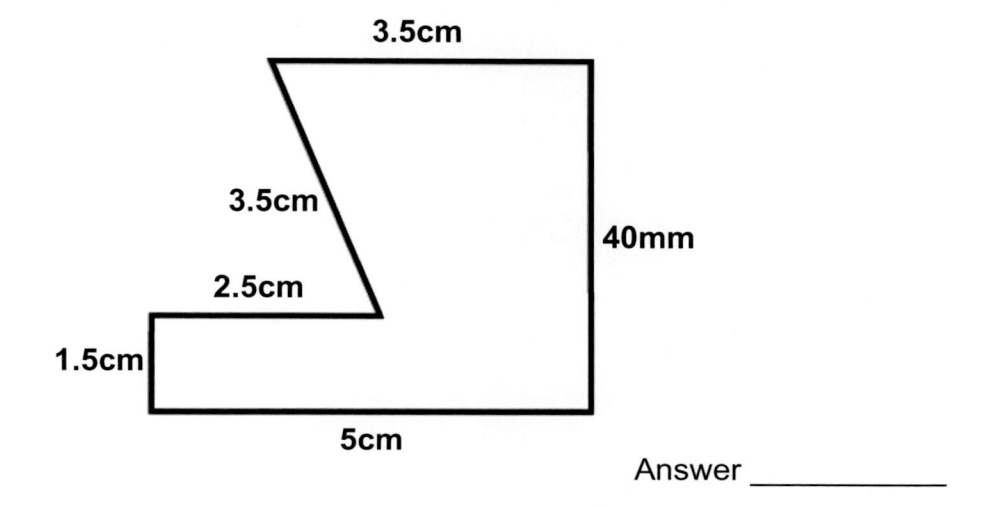

3.5cm
3.5cm
40mm
2.5cm
1.5cm
5cm

Answer _____

8) The perimeter of this shape is 1900mm, what is the value of $x$ in **mm**?

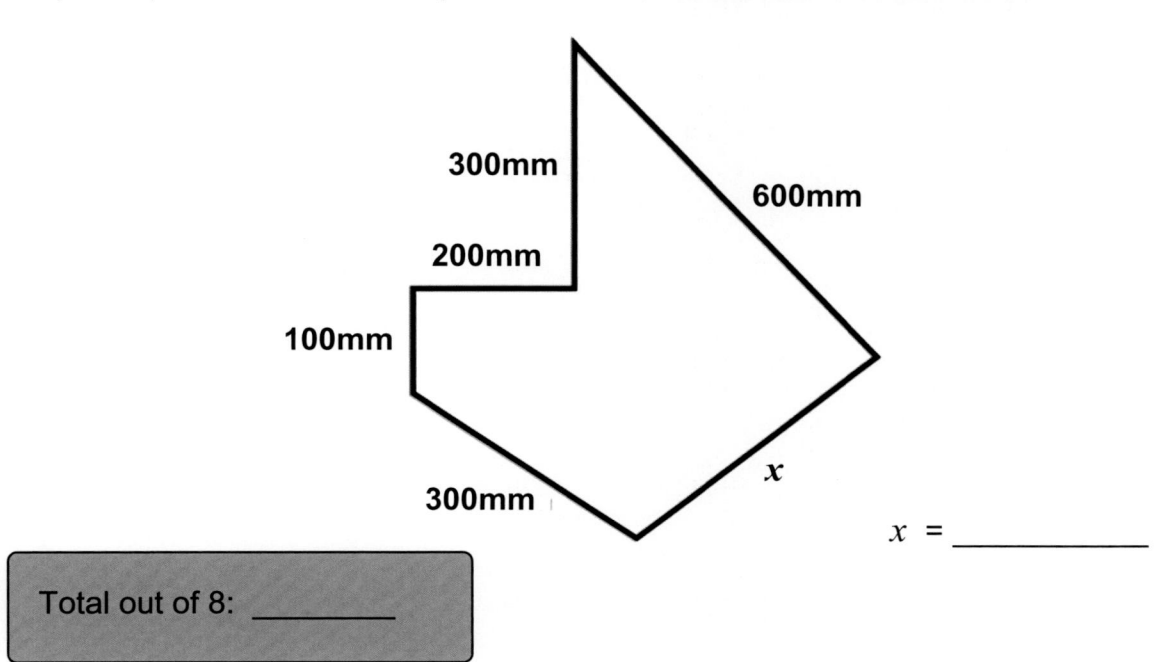

300mm
600mm
200mm
100mm
300mm
$x$

$x$ = _____

Total out of 8: _____

## Activity 3: Area

**Example:**

To work out the area of squares and rectangles use the formula:

Length x Width

[rectangle: 4cm by 2cm]

In the diagram above the length is 4cm and the width is 2cm. To find the area you would work out:

4cm x 2cm = 8 square centimetres or 8cm$^2$

When calculating area use $^2$ after the units. This can be centimetres (cm$^2$), millimetres (mm$^2$), metres (m$^2$), kilometres (km$^2$), etc.

What are the areas of the squares below?

1) [square, 4cm]

2) [square, 7cm]

3) [square, 12cm]

Answer _____     Answer _____     Answer _____

What are the areas of the rectangles below?

4)

2cm

8cm

Answer _____

5)

5cm

10cm

Answer _____

6) What is the area of this rectangle in **cm²**?

40mm

7cm

Answer _____

7) What is the area of this rectangle in **mm²**?

2cm

80mm

Answer _____

**Example:**

To work out the area of a triangle use the formula:

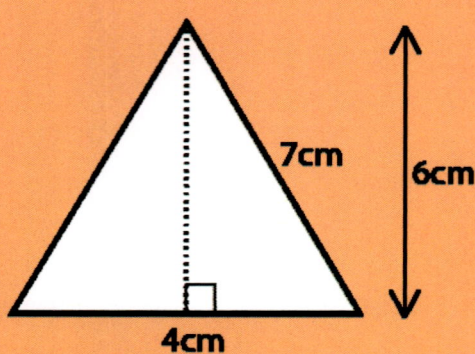

$$\frac{\text{Base} \times \text{Perpendicular height}}{2}$$

[Triangle diagram: base 4cm, slant side 7cm, perpendicular height 6cm]

You must make sure that the height used for this calculation is perpendicular to the base (the two lines meet at a right angle). The diagonal height is **not** used to work out the area.

So, to work out the area we do:

$$\frac{4 \times 6}{2} = 12\text{cm}^2$$

What are the areas of the triangles below in **cm²**?

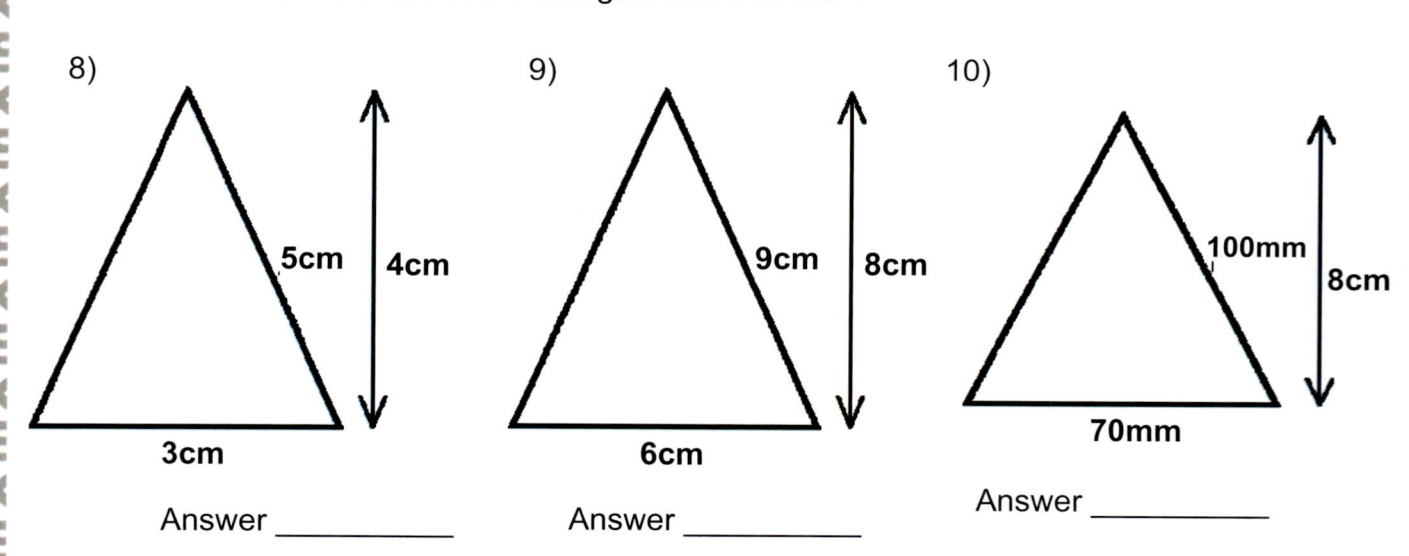

8) [Triangle: base 3cm, slant 5cm, height 4cm]

Answer _____

9) [Triangle: base 6cm, slant 9cm, height 8cm]

Answer _____

10) [Triangle: base 70mm, slant 100mm, height 8cm]

Answer _____

Total out of 10: _____

# Activity 4 – Area of Irregular Shapes

**Example:**

Irregular shapes need to be split into familiar regular shapes to work out their total area. The shape below can be split into a rectangle and a right angled triangle.

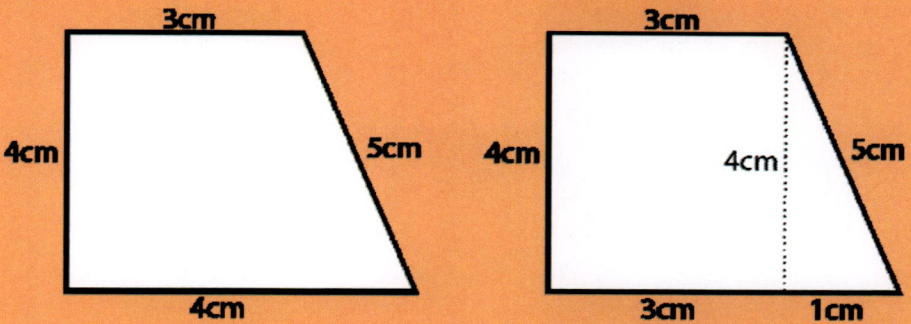

[Trapezium with top 3cm, left side 4cm, right side 5cm, bottom 4cm; split into rectangle (3cm top, 4cm height, 3cm bottom) and triangle (4cm height, 1cm base)]

Work out the area of each regular shape.
Area of rectangle = 4cm x 3cm = 12cm$^2$

Area of triangle = $\dfrac{1 \times 4}{2}$ = 2cm$^2$

Finally, add these areas together to find the area of the whole shape:

$$12 + 2 = 14\text{cm}^2$$

What are the areas of the following shapes in **cm²**?

1) [Irregular shape with measurements: 5cm, 10cm, 4cm, 9cm, 8cm, 2cm]

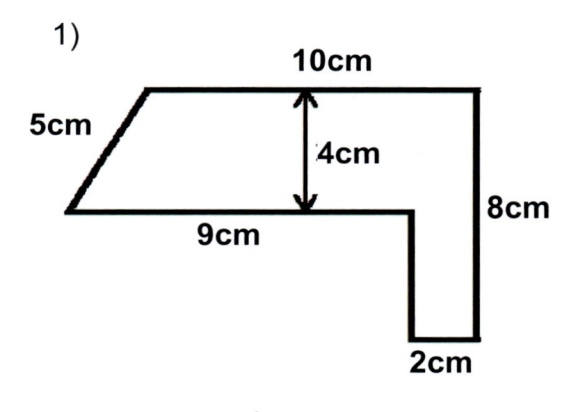

Answer _____

2) [Shape with measurements: 3cm, 2cm, 3cm, 7cm]

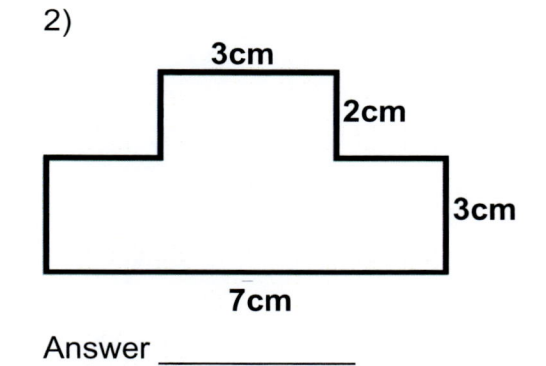

Answer _____

3) [U-shape with measurements: 3cm, 3cm, 5cm, 7cm, 10cm]

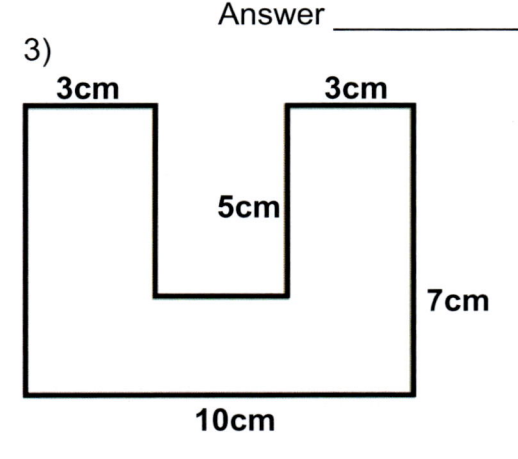

Answer _____

4) [L-shape with measurements: 1cm, 9cm, 10cm, 2cm, 2cm, 8cm]

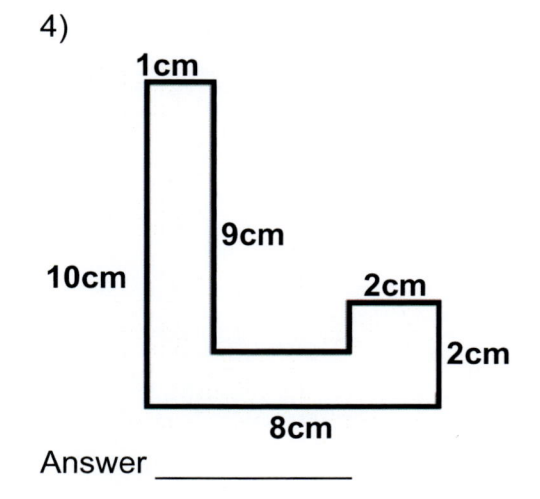

Answer _____

5) [shape with measurements: 7cm top, 2cm, 4cm, 12cm left side, 4cm, 2cm bottom]

Answer _____

6) [shape with measurements: 40mm top, 5cm, 3cm, 2cm]

Answer _____

7) [trapezium with measurements: 5cm top, 3cm, 4cm slant, 7cm bottom]

Answer _____

8) [shape with measurements: 30mm top, 4cm, 80mm, 1cm, 20mm, 3cm]

Answer _____

9) [shape with measurements: 8cm, 1cm, 1cm, 7cm left, 9cm slant, 12cm bottom]

Answer _____

10) The total area of this shape is 36cm² , what is the value of $x$ in **cm**?

[L-shape with measurements: 6cm top, 5cm, 8cm right, $x$ bottom]

Answer _____

Total out of 10: _____

## Activity 5 – Volume

**Example:**

To find the volume of cubes and cuboids, use the formula:

Length x Width x Height

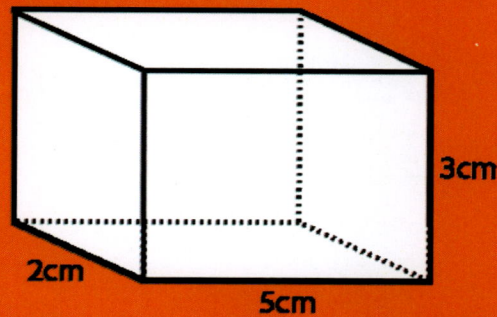

In the diagram above, the length is 5cm, the width is 2cm and the height is 3cm. Put these numbers into the formula to find out the volume of the cuboid.

5 x 2 x 3 = 30 cubic centimetres or 30cm$^3$

What are the volumes of the cubes below in **cm$^3$**?

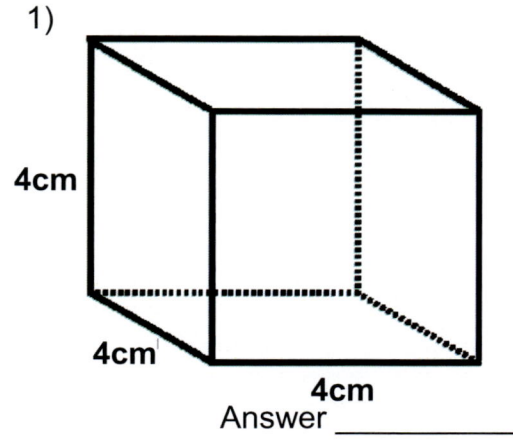

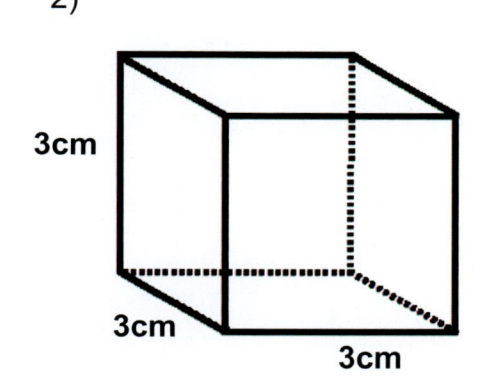

1) 4cm, 4cm, 4cm
Answer _____

2) 3cm, 3cm, 3cm
Answer _____

3) 5cm, 5cm, 5cm
Answer _____

4) 10mm
Answer _____

What are the volumes of the cuboids below in **cm³**?

5)

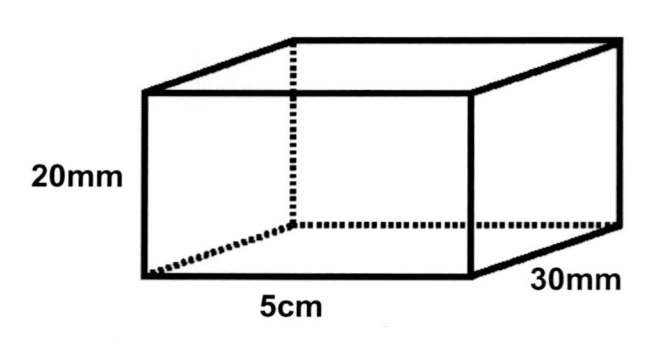

20mm
5cm
30mm

Answer _____

6)

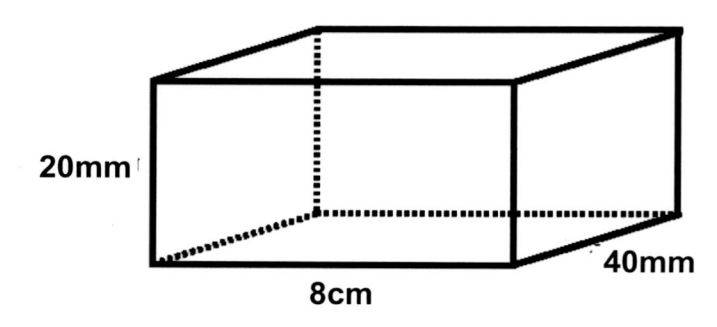

20mm
8cm
40mm

Answer _____

7) The volume of this cuboid is 150 cm³, find the length of side *x* in **cm**.

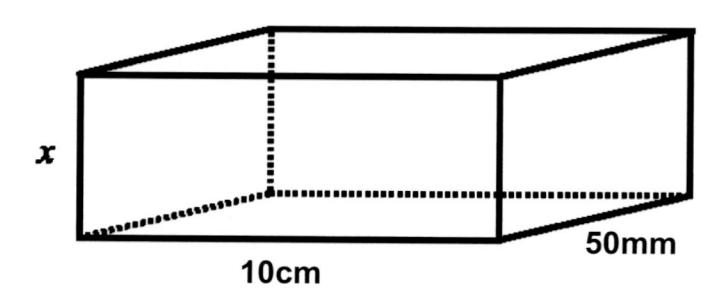

*x*
10cm
50mm

Answer _____

**Example**:

The formula for finding the volume of a triangular prism is:

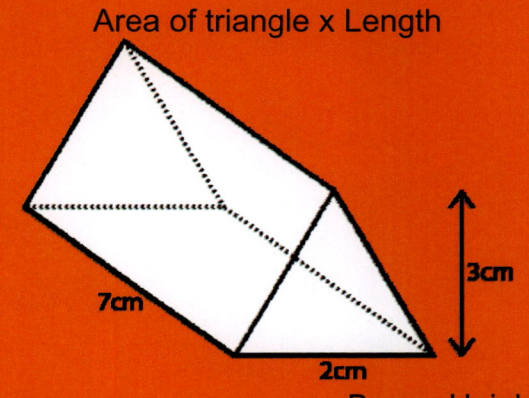

Area of triangle x Length

Find the area of a triangle using the formula $\frac{\text{Base} \times \text{Height}}{2}$, then multiply your answer by the length.

$$\text{Area of triangle} = \frac{2 \times 3}{2} = 3\text{cm}^2$$

Volume of prism = 3 x 7 = 21cm³

What are the volumes of the triangular prisms below in **cm³**.

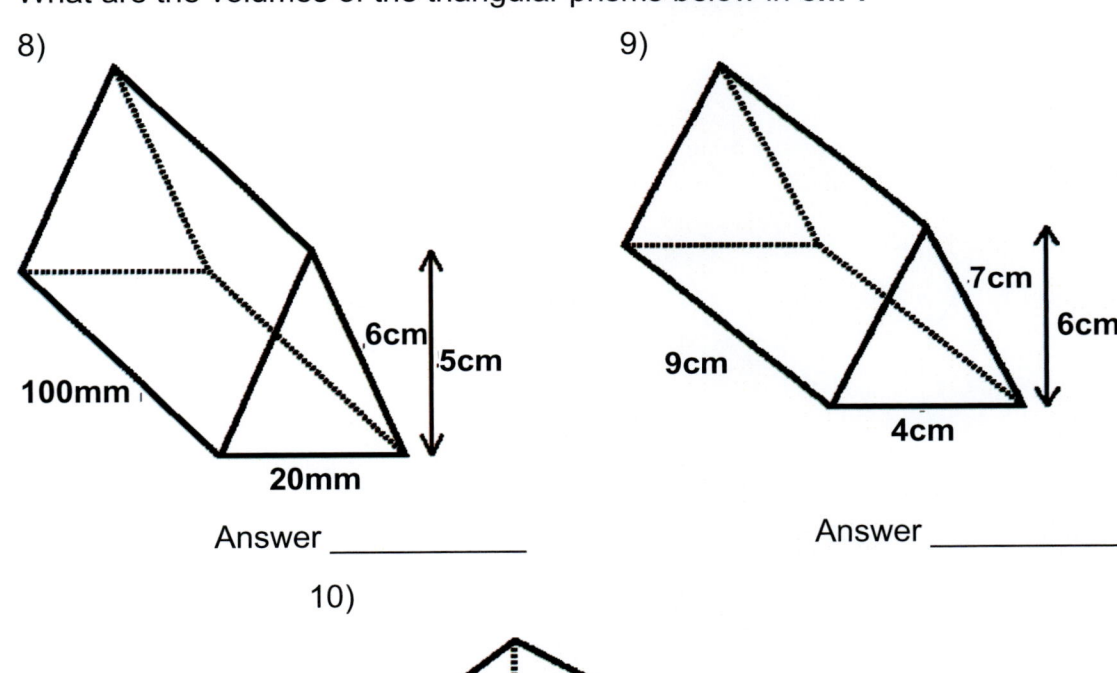

8) 100mm, 20mm, 6cm, 5cm

Answer _____

9) 9cm, 4cm, 7cm, 6cm

Answer _____

10) 3cm, 7cm, 5cm

Answer _____

Total out of 10: _____

# Activity 6 – Surface Area

**Example:**

The surface area of a shape is found by calculating the total area of all the faces.

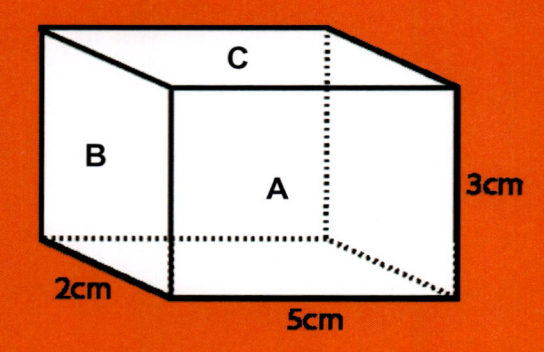

[Cuboid diagram with faces labelled A, B, C and dimensions 2cm, 5cm, 3cm]

The diagram above shows a cuboid. It has three pairs of identical faces. You must work out the area of each different face and then multiply it by 2.

Area of A = 5 x 3 = 15cm$^2$ x 2 = 30cm$^2$
Area of B = 2 x 3 =  6cm$^2$ x 2 = 12cm$^2$
Area of C = 2 x 5 = 10cm$^2$ x 2 = 20cm$^2$

Finally, add up these values to find the total surface area.
30 + 12 + 20 = 62cm$^2$

*Note: With a cube you can find the area of one face and multiply it by 6 to find the total surface area.*

What are the surface area values of the shapes below? Write your answers in **cm$^2$**.

1) [Cube with sides 3cm, 3cm, 3cm]

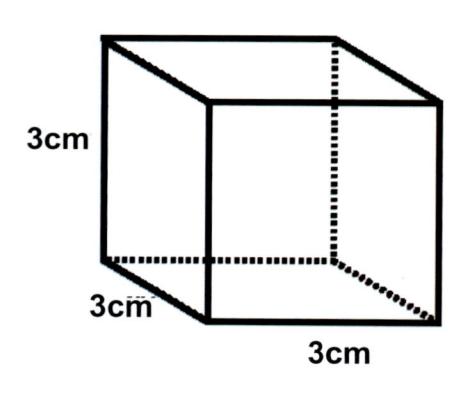

Answer _____

2) [Cube with sides 4cm, 4cm, 4cm]

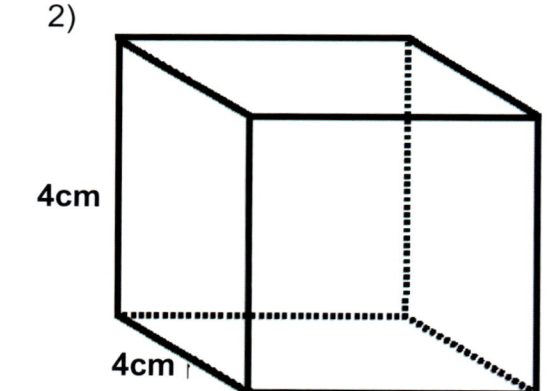

Answer _____

# AREA, PERIMETER AND VOLUME ANSWER BOOKLET

- This booklet includes answers to the Area, Perimeter and Volume pack.

- One mark is awarded for each correct answer unless stated otherwise within the instructions for each activity.

- Once you have marked an activity, you can insert the percentage into the space provided at the back of the book.

- After an activity has been marked, go through any incorrect answers, ensuring your child understands what the correct answer is and why.

# Perimeter, Area and Volume Answers

### Activity 1

**Perimeter**

1. 20cm
2. 30cm
3. 40cm
4. 30cm
5. 24cm
6. 16cm
7. 36cm
8. 34cm
9. 46cm
10. 37cm
11. 42cm

### Activity 2

**Perimeter and Missing measurements**

1. 50cm
2. 32cm
3. 38cm
4. x = 5cm
5. x = 6cm
6. x = 2.5cm
7. 20cm
8. 400mm

### Activity 3

**Area**

1. 16cm$^2$
2. 49cm$^2$
3. 144cm$^2$
4. 16cm$^2$
5. 50cm$^2$
6. 28cm$^2$
7. 1600mm$^2$
8. 6cm$^2$
9. 24cm$^2$
10. 28cm$^2$

### Activity 4

**Area of Irregular shapes**

1. 50cm$^2$
2. 27cm$^2$
3. 50cm$^2$
4. 19cm$^2$
5. 40cm$^2$
6. 34cm$^2$
7. 18cm$^2$
8. 23cm$^2$
9. 74.5cm$^2$
10. x = 2cm

# Perimeter, Area and Volume Answers

### Activity 5

**Volume**

1. $64cm^3$
2. $27cm^3$
3. $125cm^3$
4. $1cm^3$
5. $30cm^3$
6. $64cm^3$
7. $3cm$
8. $50cm^3$
9. $108cm^3$
10. $52.5cm^3$

### Activity 6

**Surface Area**

1. $54cm^2$
2. $96cm^2$
3. $150cm^2$
4. $236cm^2$
5. $108cm^2$
6. $238cm^2$
7. $430cm^2$
8. $86m^2$
9. $111cm^2$
10. $204m^2$

### Activity 7

**Area and Perimeter**

1. P = 28cm, A = $49cm^2$
2. P = 25cm, A = $25cm^2$
3. P = 22cm, A = $24cm^2$
4. P = 13cm, A = $6cm^2$
5. P = 16cm, A = $8cm^2$
6. P = 26cm, A = $32cm^2$
7. P = 38cm, A = $42cm^2$
8. P = 66cm, A = $108cm^2$
9. $x$ = 4cm, P = 42cm
10. P = 40cm, A = $68cm^2$

### Activity 8

**Perimeter – word problems**

1. P = 23.5m. Yes she can have an extension
2. P = 142cm
3. P = 19.5m
4. P = 6m
5. 20.2m
6. 330cm
7. 10.1m
8. 6 posters
9. 12.5m
10. $x$ = 800cm, P = 2720cm

## Activity 9

### Area and volume – word problems

1. SA = 2200cm$^2$
   V = 6000cm$^3$
   NO new lunch box
2. 626cm$^2$
3. 1264cm$^2$
4. a) 726cm$^2$
   b) 2904cm$^2$
5. SA = 1130cm$^2$
   V = 1650cm$^3$
6. 5 games
7. a) 40400cm$^2$ ($x$ = 160cm)
   b) 2076cm$^2$ (Surface area of cuboid = 1244cm$^2$ and surface area of prism = 832cm$^2$)
   c) 5712cm$^3$ (Volume of cuboid = 3808cm$^3$ and volume of prism = 1904cm$^3$)

## Activity 10

### Perimeter, area and volume – word problems

1. a) 48 panels
   b) 165 bricks
   c) $x$ = 25cm
   Surface Area = 1060cm$^2$
2. a) 504m$^2$
   b) 80m
   c) 201.6m$^3$
3. C (A = 5890cm$^2$, B = 5600cm$^2$, C = 5950cm$^2$, D = 8400cm$^2$)
4. a) 6 metres
   b) 3200cm$^2$
   c) 67200cm$^3$

3) 

5cm
5cm
5cm

Answer _____

4)

5cm
8cm
6cm

Answer _____

5)

3cm
0.06m
4cm

Answer _____

6)

0.04m
11cm
0.05m

Answer _____

**Example:**

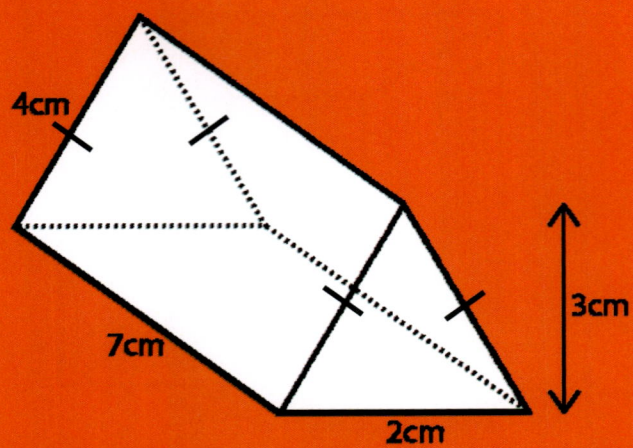

The surface area of a prism is found by calculating the area of each face and adding them together. There may be some identical faces, such as the triangular faces here, which can be calculated once and then doubled. The calculations will look like this:

$$\text{Area of triangle: } \frac{2 \times 3}{2} = 3cm^2 \times 2 = 6cm^2$$

$$\text{Area of sides: } 4 \times 7 = 28cm^2 \times 2 = 56cm^2$$

$$\text{Area of base: } 2 \times 7 = 14cm^2 \times 1 = 14cm^2$$

Finally, add up these values to find the total surface area.
$$56 + 14 + 6 = 76cm^2$$

What are the surface areas of the following triangular prisms?

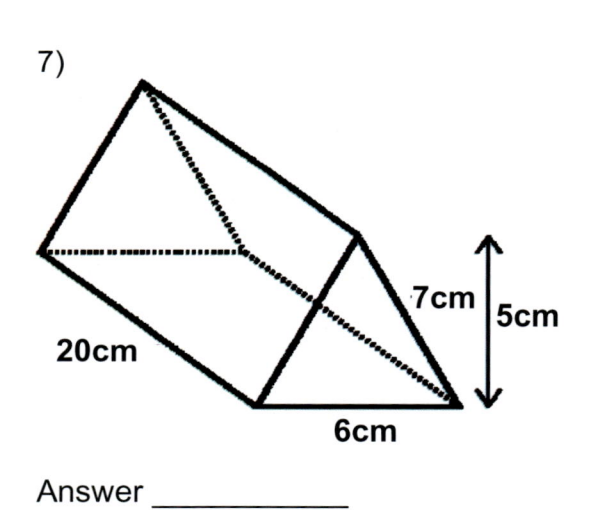

7)

Answer _____

8)

Answer _____

9)

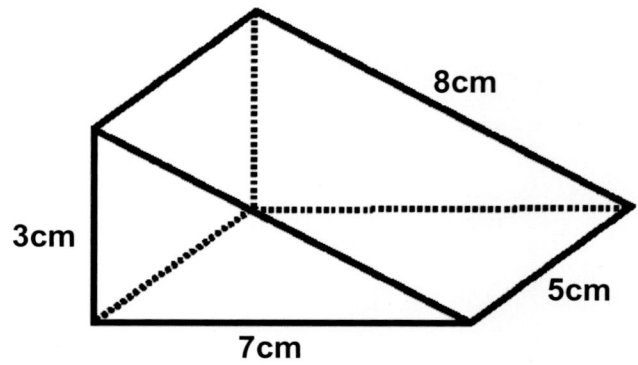

3cm, 8cm, 5cm, 7cm

Answer _____

10)

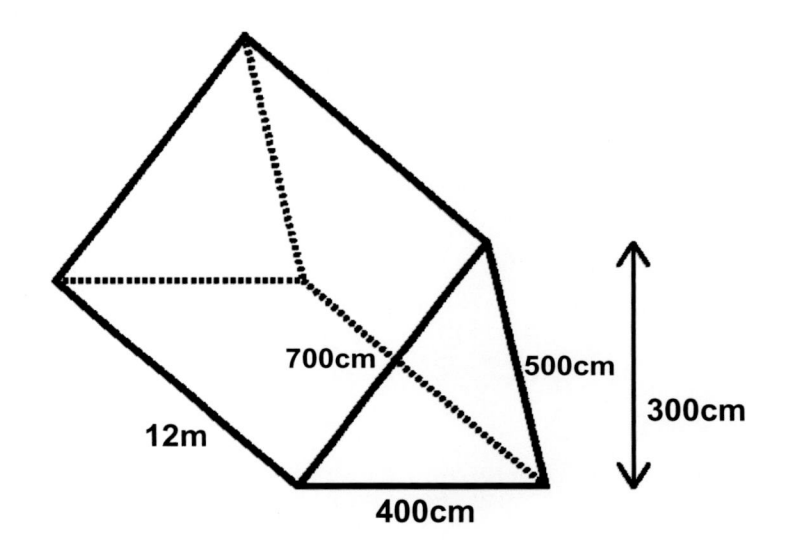

700cm, 500cm, 300cm, 12m, 400cm

Answer _____

Total out of 10: _____

## Activity 7 – Area and Perimeter

1) What is the area and perimeter of this square?

7cm

Perimeter _____ Area _____

What are the area (**cm²**) and perimeter (**cm**) values for the shapes below?

2)

2.5cm

10cm

Perimeter _____ Area _____

3)

3cm

80mm

Perimeter _____ Area _____

4)

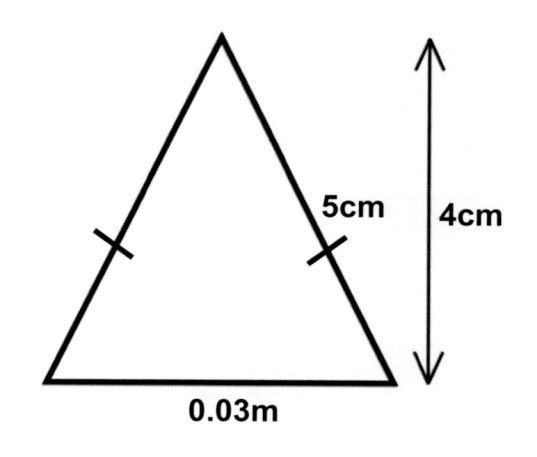

[Triangle with slant side 5cm, height 4cm, base 0.03m]

Perimeter _____  Area _____

5)

[Triangle with slant side 0.06m, height 4cm, base 0.04m]

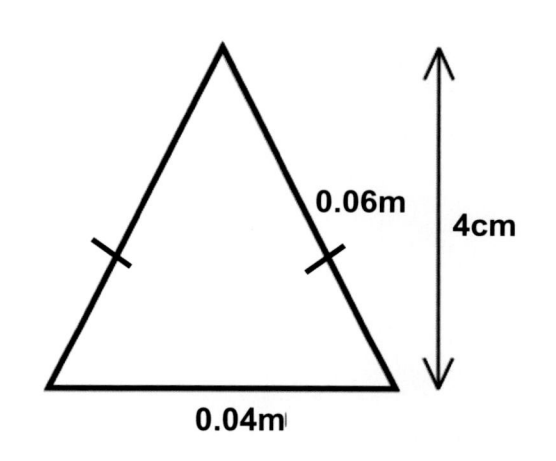

Perimeter _____  Area _____

What are the area (**cm²**) and perimeter (**cm**) values for the shapes below?

6)

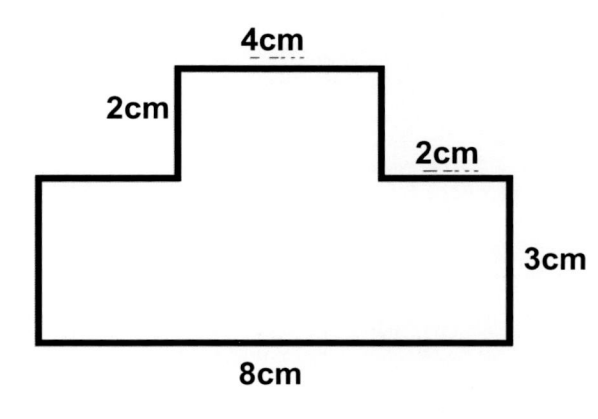

[T-shaped figure: top 4cm, 2cm, 2cm, 3cm, 8cm base]

Perimeter _____  Area _____

7)

3cm, 5cm, 3cm, 6cm, 2cm

Perimeter _____ Area _____

8)

3cm, 3cm, 9cm, 150mm, 9cm

Perimeter _____ Area _____

9) The total area of this shape is 84cm², what is the value of $x$? Then find the perimeter of the shape.

12cm, 6cm, 9cm, $x$

$x =$ _____

Perimeter _____

10) What is the area (**cm²**) and perimeter (**cm**) of this shape?

60mm, 80mm, 4cm, 2cm

Perimeter _____

Area _____

Total out of 20: _____

## Activity 8 – Perimeter: Word Problems

1) Below is a plan of Katie's bedroom. She wants an extension but her dad thinks her room is already big enough. He tells Katie that if the perimeter of her bedroom is less than 25m, she can have an extension. Can Katie have an extension?

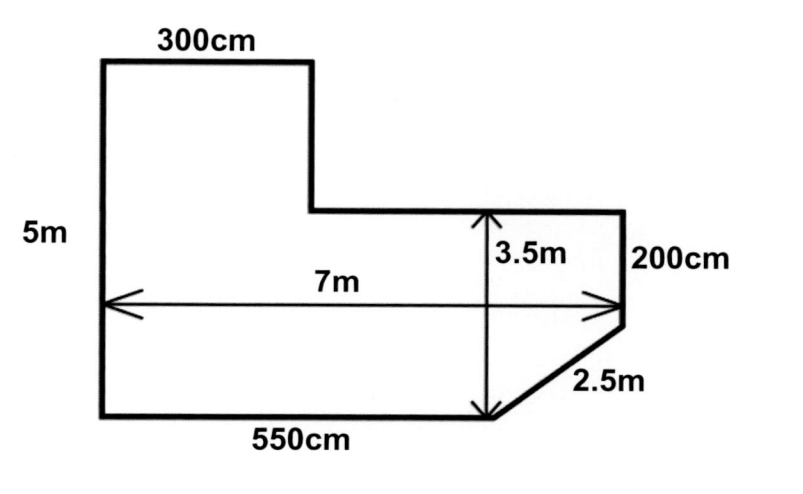

*(Diagram: L-shaped room with dimensions 300cm (top), 5m (left side), 7m (horizontal middle), 3.5m (vertical middle), 200cm (right side), 2.5m (diagonal), 550cm (bottom))*

Perimeter = _____ metres

Does Katie get her extension?   **YES / NO**

2) Simon has a new computer monitor and wants to find the perimeter of the screen. The dimensions of the screen are 2cm smaller than the dimensions of the frame. Find the perimeter of the screen in **cm**.

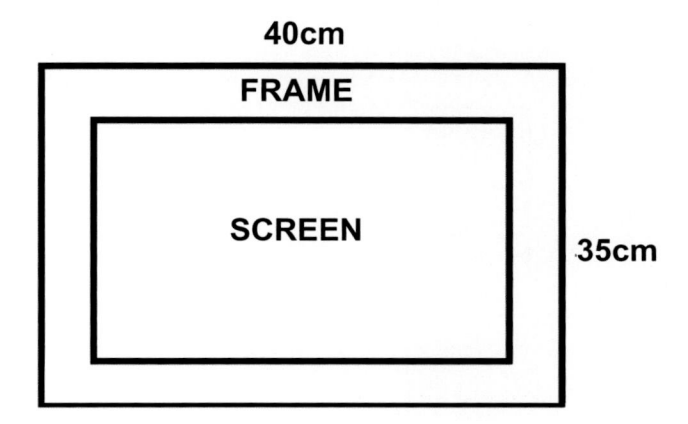

*(Diagram: Frame labelled 40cm across the top and 35cm down the right side, with SCREEN inside.)*

Answer _____

3) Max plans to make a gravel border to go around his lawn. He draws a plan of his garden and records all the measurements. How long will his gravel border be in metres?

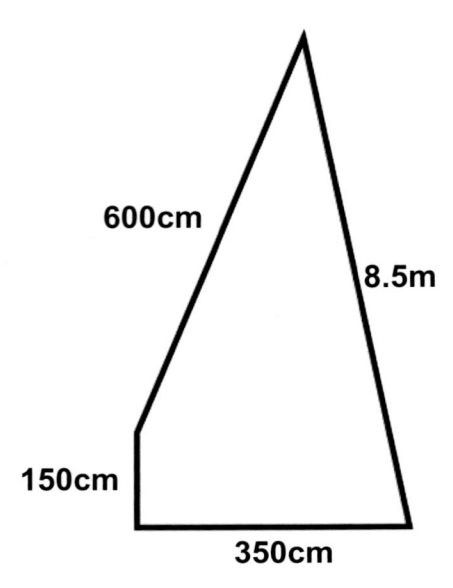

600cm
8.5m
150cm
350cm

Answer _____

4) Sakura is digging a new vegetable patch using the plan below. She allows 0.8m for each row of vegetables. The perimeter of the vegetable patch is triple the size of the previous patch. What was the perimeter of the previous vegetable patch in metres?

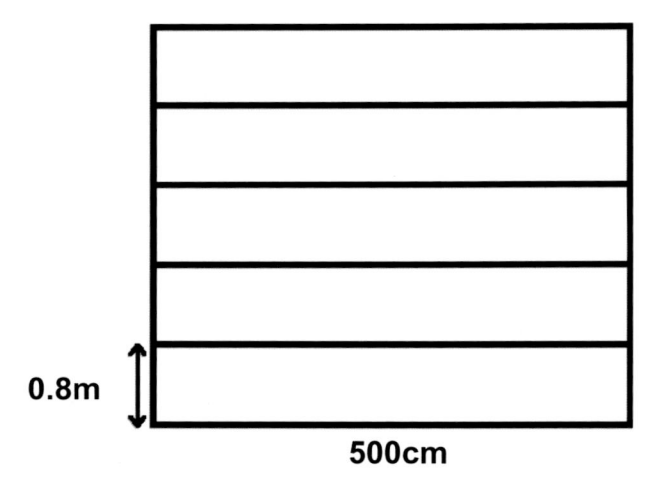

0.8m
500cm

Answer _____

5) John sets up a fitness circuit in his garden and maps out the path he has to run around. The set of cones map out a regular hexagon and a square joined together by a straight line. From the black cone, John runs in a clockwise direction around the hexagon, along the straight line, around the square and back to the black cone. What is the length of the path that John has to cover in metres?

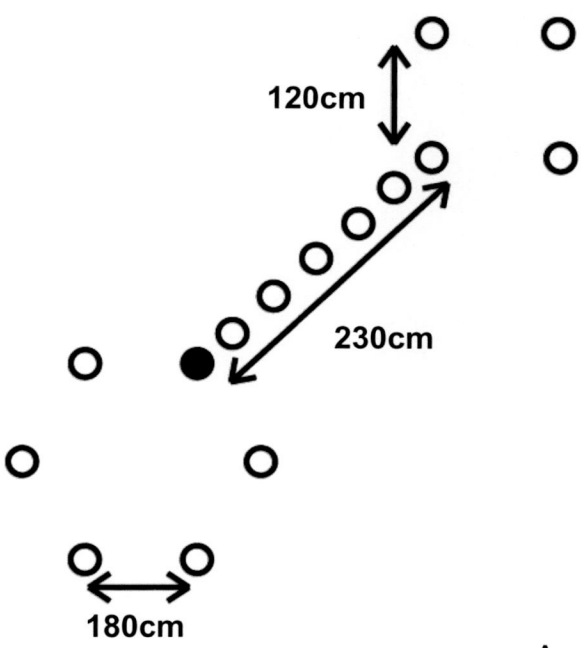

120cm

230cm

180cm

Answer _____

6) Alice wants to buy a new frame for her painting project. The frame has measurements which are all 10cm longer than her original frame. Below is her original frame. Find the perimeter of her new frame in **cm**.

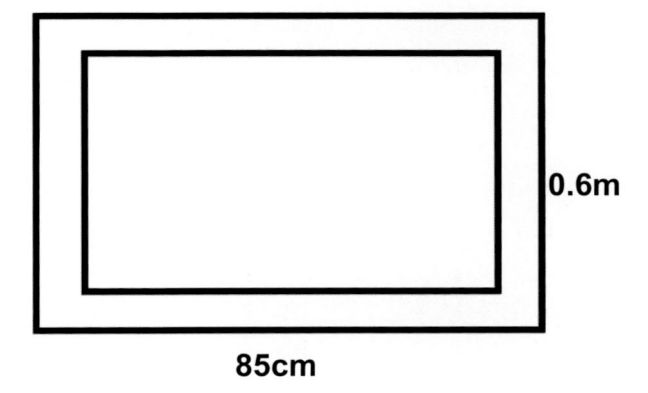

0.6m

85cm

Answer _____

7) Simon wants to rearrange the furniture in his living room. He moves his television away from the wall socket, so he needs to run a power cable around the room to plug it in. The cable needs to go exactly half way round the room. What will the length of the cable be in metres?

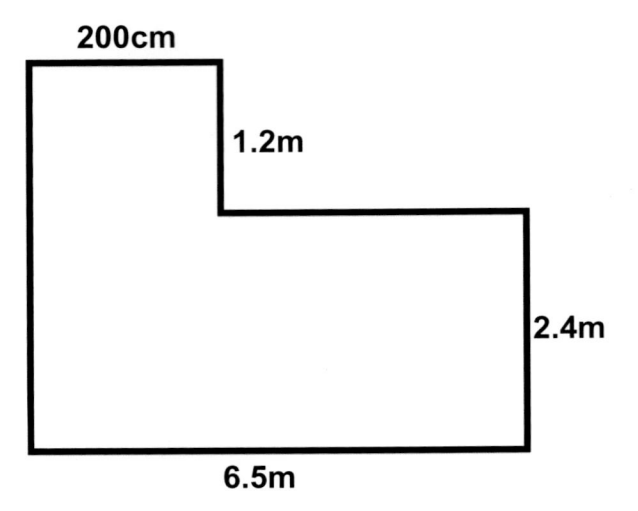

200cm

1.2m

2.4m

6.5m

Answer _____

8) Edward wants to decorate one of his bedroom walls with some posters and wants to work out how many posters he can put up. Each poster is 70cm wide. Below is a plan of his bedroom. The wall labelled $x$ is where he wants his posters. If the perimeter of his bedroom is 2040cm, how many posters will he get going along the wall labelled $x$?

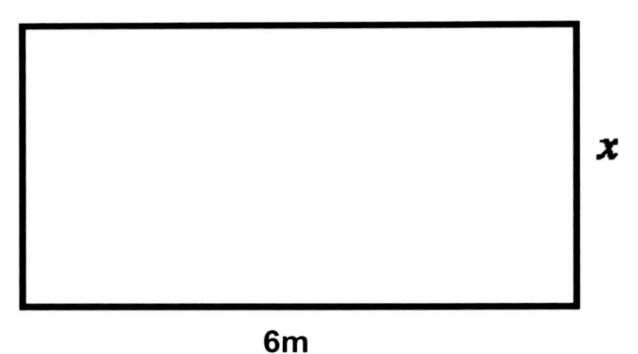

$x$

6m

Answer _____

9) Arthur is doing some gardening with his cousin Lance. They dig around the edges of the garden and pick out the weeds. By the end of the day they have weeded half way around the edge of the garden. How far have they weeded in metres?

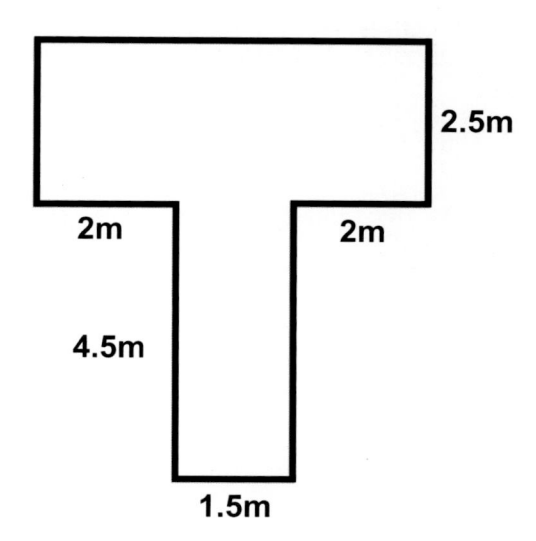

2.5m

2m    2m

4.5m

1.5m

Answer _____

10) Thomas wants to buy new paving stones to put around his swimming pool. Each paving stone is 40cm long and 40cm wide. Below shows the size of the pool. The perimeter of the pool is 2400cm. Work out $x$ in cms and what the new perimeter will be including the paving stones.

400cm

$x$

$x = $ _____

New Perimeter _____

Total out of 12: _____

## Activity 9 – Area and Volume: Word Problems

1) Carlton needs a new lunchbox for school. His mum thinks that it needs to have a surface area of at least 2400cm$^2$ and a volume of less than 5000cm$^3$. He chooses his favourite lunchbox at the shop. The dimensions are given below. Can Carlton have this lunch box?

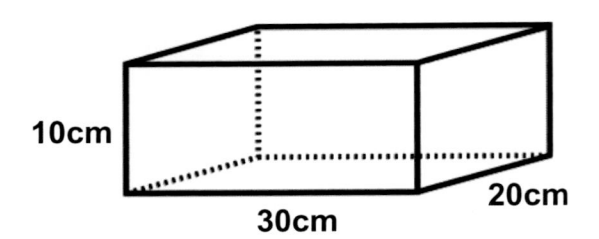

   10cm, 30cm, 20cm

   Surface Area _____    Volume _____

   Can Carlton have the lunch box?  **YES / NO**

2) A chocolate brownie company are designing a new packet for their brownies. The new packet will have a volume of 660cm$^3$. What is the surface area of the packet? Give your answer in **cm$^2$**.

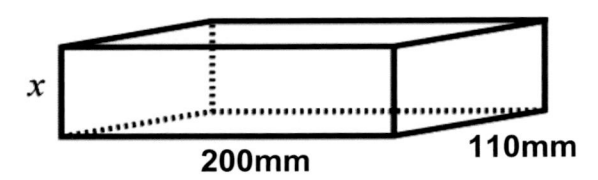

   $x$, 200mm, 110mm

   Answer _____

3) Rei is wrapping up a present for her friend. She knows that to wrap the present neatly she will need 400cm$^2$ extra than the total surface area. How much paper (**cm$^2$**) will she need to wrap the present?

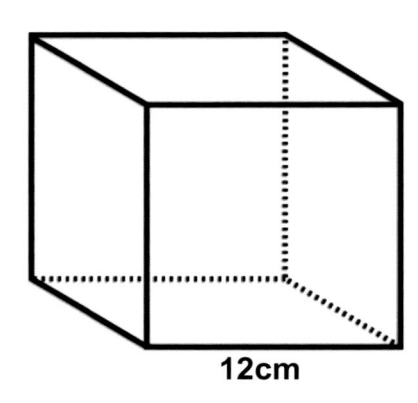

   12cm

   Answer _____

4) A building cube has an edge of 11cm.

   a) What is its surface area?

   Answer _____

   b) If 8 of these cubes are used to build a bigger cube, what will the surface area of the bigger cube be?

   Answer _____

5) Samantha buys a chocolate bar for her sister. The chocolate bar is a triangular prism and is fairly long. The diagram below shows the dimensions of the bar. Use this information to find the surface area ($cm^2$) and volume ($cm^3$) of the chocolate bar.

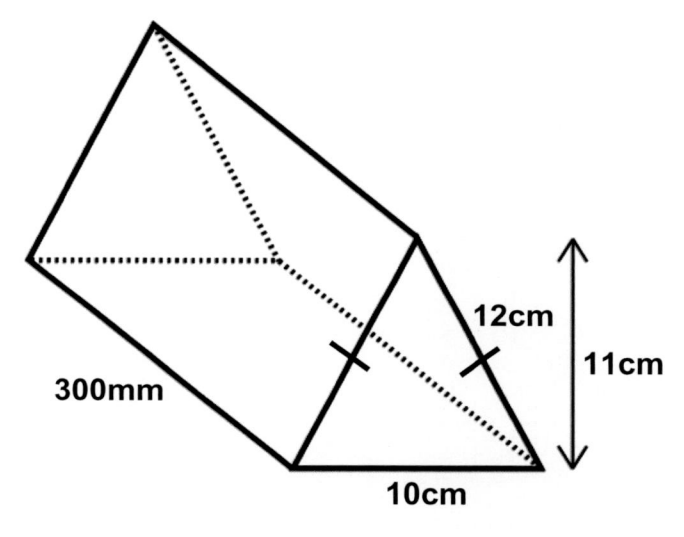

   (Triangular prism: length 300mm, triangular face with sides 12cm, 10cm, and height 11cm)

   Surface Area _____  Volume _____

6) Lucy buys a new storage container for her board games. Each board game has a volume of 33600$cm^3$. Find out how many board games can be stored in her container.

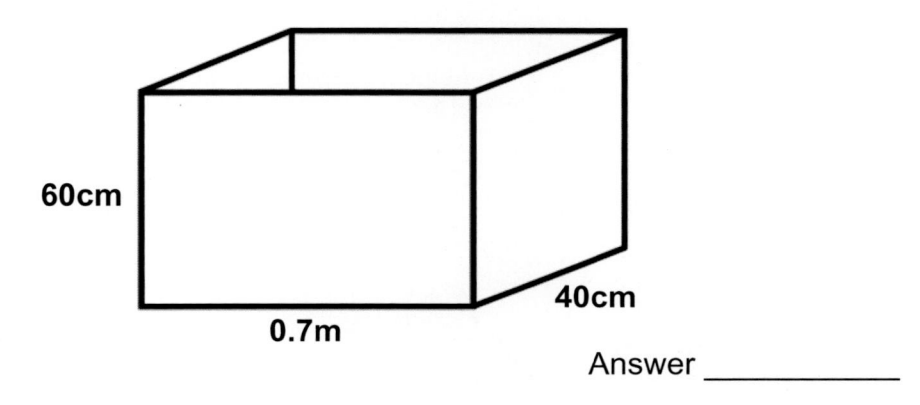

   (Box dimensions: 60cm height, 40cm width, 0.7m length)

   Answer _____

7) A skate ramp is being constructed for Tyson and his friends. It has a volume of 416000cm³. It is Tyson's job to buy enough paint to cover it. The boys must work out how much of the ramp needs painting. They have decided to paint all the sides except for the base.

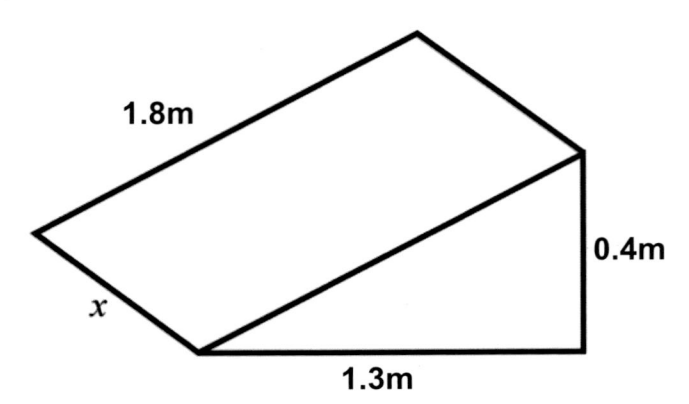

a) What is the surface area that needs painting in **cm²**?

Answer _____

Tyson built a model of his ideal ramp.

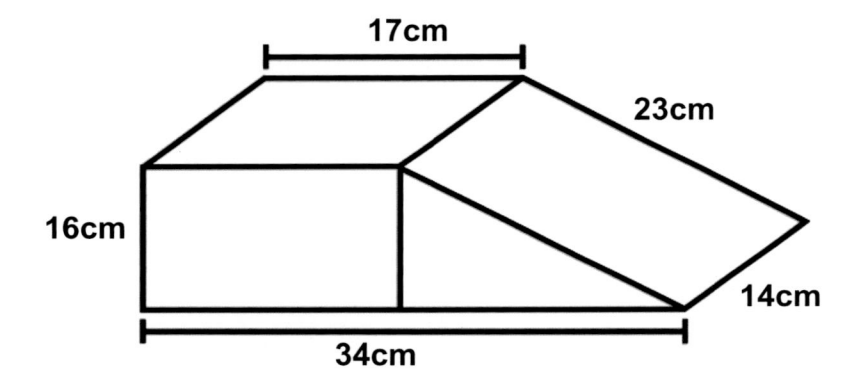

Find:
b) The total surface area of the ramp model.

Answer _____

c) The volume of the ramp model.

Answer _____

Total out of 13: _____

## Activity 10 – Perimeter, Area and Volume: Word Problems

1) Rishi wants to build a new fence around his garden. He needs to know the perimeter of his garden in order to buy the correct number of fence panels. Each panel has a length of 1.25m.

   a) How many whole panels would Rishi need to buy in order to cover the perimeter of the entire garden?

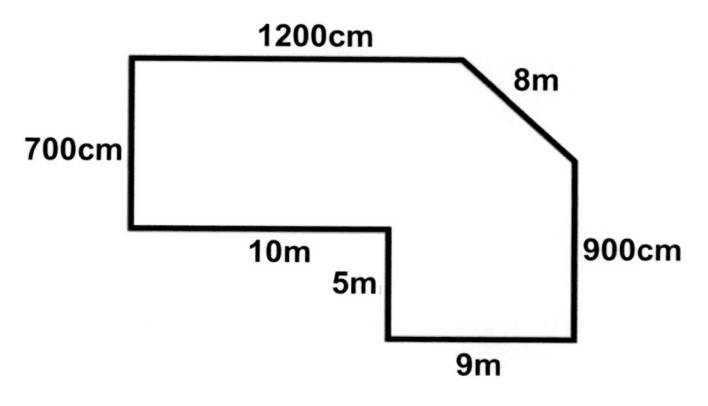

   (Shape with sides: 1200cm, 8m, 700cm, 10m, 5m, 900cm, 9m)

   Answer _____

Rishi then wants to buy some bricks to build a summer house in the garden. The bricks are stored in crates and each brick has a volume of 2000cm$^3$. The dimensions for the crates are shown below.

   b) How many bricks can be stored in each crate?

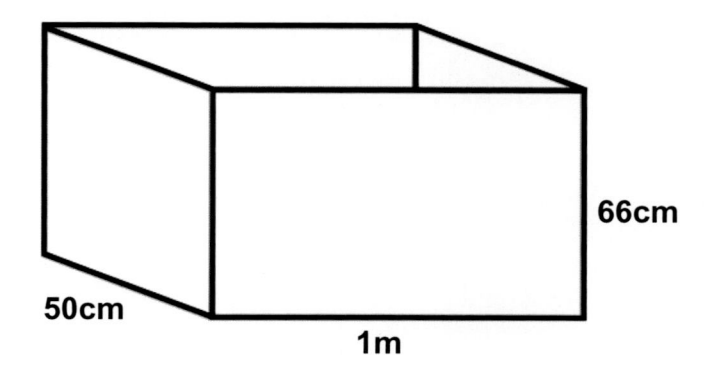

   (Crate dimensions: 50cm, 1m, 66cm)

   Answer _____

The diagram below shows the dimensions of one brick, which has a volume of 2000cm³.

c) What is the value of $x$ and what is the surface area of the brick?

8cm
10cm
$x$

$x$ _____          Surface area _____

2. A school is having a concrete basketball court constructed for the children. The dimensions for the concrete area required are 28m long and 18m wide.

   a) Find the area of the concrete court.

   Answer _____

The lines of the basketball court need to be painted onto the concrete. There will be a 1.5 metre border inside the edge of the concrete.

   b) What is the perimeter of the basketball court?

   Answer _____

The depth of the hole for the concrete to fill is 40cm.

   c) What will the volume of the concrete be? Give your answer in m³.

   Answer _____

3. Marcus is buying a new desk for work. His old desk had an area of 5000cm². He decides that the new desk needs to have an area close to 6000cm².

   Which of the following desks should he choose? Circle your answer.

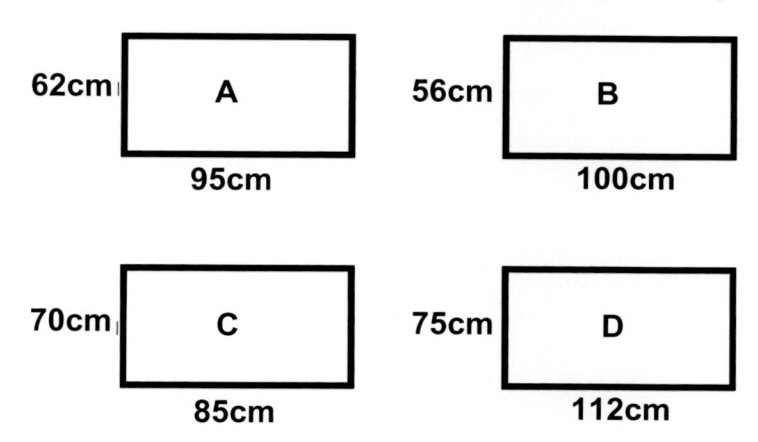

   62cm | A | 95cm

   56cm | B | 100cm

   70cm | C | 85cm

   75cm | D | 112cm

4. Drake is getting a pet lizard. The lizard will live in a glass tank which is shown below.

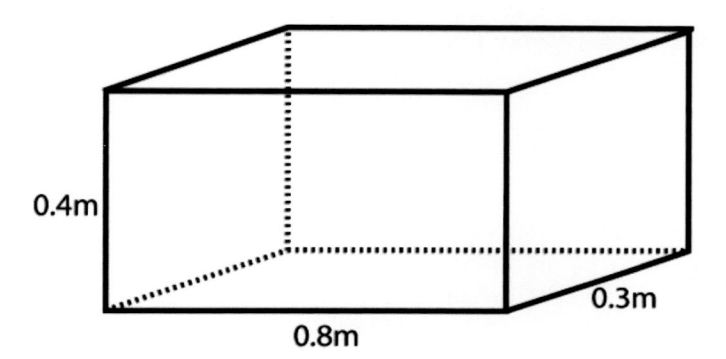

   0.4m, 0.8m, 0.3m

   a) What is the perimeter of the tank in meters?

   Answer _____

   Drake is going to attach a background picture to the tank. The picture will be fixed to one of the larger sides of the tank and it will fill the entire side.

   b) What will the area of the background picture be in **cm²**?

   Answer _____

   The bottom of the tank will be filled with sand for the lizard to walk on. The tank will be filled 12cm high.

   c) What will the volume of empty space left in the tank be in **cm³**?

   Answer _____

   Total out of 11: _____

## Success Record

Use the empty bar graph below to record your child's score for each activity so their progress can be tracked. Work out the percentage for each activity and draw the bar onto the graph.

**Percentage** (y-axis: 0 to 100 in increments of 10)
**Activity Number** (x-axis: 1 to 10)